REVERIE

FLOATING BETWEEN DREAMS AND REALITY.

RENA TARA PHOOKAN

to my mother, who pushes me to be the best me,

to my father, who shows me i can exist happily in every version of me,

to my grandfathers, who, although gone, guide me and inspire me every
single day of my life.

to dreamers, believers, and those of little faith.

to those who *feel.*

Contents

Contents

Foreword

There are books that speak, and then there are books that hum—softly, intimately, like a secret meant just for you. Reverie is the latter. It is a collection of longing and memory, of love and loss, of the quiet ache that lingers between what was and what could have been.

These poems do not ask for permission; they simply settle into your bones, weaving themselves into the spaces you thought were empty. They are raw, tender, and unapologetically human—a reflection of what it means to feel deeply, to dream endlessly, to hold on even as you learn to let go.

This is not just a book. It is a heartbeat, a sigh, a fleeting dream you'll want to return to again and again.

Preface

This is a book for the ones who have lived inside their own heads too long. For the ones who have spent nights staring at the ceiling, drowning in questions that have no answers. For the ones who have tried to grasp at something—love, belonging, certainty—only to watch it slip through their fingers like water.

Reverie is a collection of everything I have held close and everything I have had to let go. It is the weight of leaving and the ache of staying. It is the quiet loneliness of growing up, of realizing that effort does not always lead to reward, that home is not always a place, that some things are meant to remain unfinished.

These poems are for the dreamers, the ones who feel too much, who carry the past like an old song humming beneath their skin. They are for the ones who have measured their worth in numbers, in achievements, in expectations too heavy to bear. For the ones who have loved and lost, who have searched and still not found.

This is not a book of answers. It is a book of echoes, of memories, of the fleeting moments that make us human.

So read, and let yourself feel. Let yourself drift. Let yourself dream.

Welcome to Reverie.

Acknowledgements

This book would not exist without the love, patience, and unwavering support of so many people who have shaped me, held me, and believed in me even when I struggled to believe in myself.

To my **family**—thank you for grounding me, for being my safe place, for always reminding me where I come from. Your love is woven into every word of this book.

To my friends—the ones who have listened to my late-night ramblings, who have held my hand through heartbreaks and dreams alike, who have made life feel a little less lonely. This book is for you.

To every teacher, mentor and kind soul who ever encouraged me to keep writing—you have no idea the impact your words have had on me.

To my readers—thank you for stepping into this world with me, for feeling these words, for making them your own.

And finally, to Notion Press—thank you for giving my words a home. For helping me bring this collection to life, for making the dream of holding my own book in my hands a reality. I am endlessly grateful.

This book is a piece of my heart. Thank you for holding it with me.

Prologue

Dreams exist in the spaces between—between waking and sleeping, between memory and possibility, between the past we carry and the future we chase. Reverie is born from those in-between moments, where longing lingers like a half-remembered melody and love—whether lost, unspoken, or burning bright—leaves its mark on the soul.

These poems are echoes of what was and what could have been. They are the wildfire of desire, the hush of grief, the quiet persistence of hope. They are the unspoken words, the almosts, the infinite possibilities folded into the corners of the universe.

To read Reverie is to step into a world where emotions do not ask for permission—they simply are. Where love, loss, wonder, and yearning blur together like colors on a canvas. This is a collection for those who feel deeply, who dream endlessly, who know what it is to carry a universe within them.

So step in. Wander. Remember. Dream.

1. the airport.

the girl with the fluorescent yellow backpack grins from ear to ear, finally heading home after a long semester at uni.
the boy with the sunglasses poses for a selfie, he's getting ready for a bachelor's weekend with his best friends.
the lady with smile lines and delicate wrinkles framing her forehead smiles fondly at her granddaughter, she's visiting her hometown for the first time in twenty years.

the man in the navy suit waits by the boarding gate, earphones plugged in as he barks instructions to his secretary.
his usually crisp shirt is crumpled, the soft cotton of his handkerchief is scrunched tightly in his fist.
his mother is sick. he's heading home to see her for the last time.
the girl with the bright red lipstick cries in the corner because her best friend is finally marrying the love of her life and she's going to the wedding. shes a bridesmaid.

the woman with greying hair and   kind eyes looks out the window, phone open to the gallery app.
there's a picture of her as a little girl with a handsome man beside her, her father, strong and tall, grinning ear to ear
shes going home for his funeral.
a young boy sits quietly, fingers crossed and headphones playing a soft melody as he looks at the planes taxing on the runway.

he's leaving for his first ever semester at uni. for the first time, he's flying solo.

he's anxious. but he's starting a brand new adventure.

a baby stands on wobbly legs, hands pressed against the cold glass, eyes agape in wonder and awe as she takes in the sparkling lights.

shes excited to fly.

a young couple, with matching silver rings on their fingers and contagious laughter, grip onto each other's hands tightly.

they're heading for their honeymoon. preparing for decades of togetherness.

im sitting on a chair in the very last row of seats.

im heading home with my mother after a mother daughter trip.

im caught up in my own thoughts, too busy thinking about myself and how im going to make a name for myself in the future

im sitting on a chair in the very last row of seats.

im writing my own story.

and all around me, everyone else is living out theirs.

2. a recipe for overwhelm.

200 grams of butter—did I finish my task?
150 grams sugar—time's slipping too fast.
3 eggs in the bowl, my paper's still due,
one night to complete it—I have to simply power through.
a cup and a half full of fine-milled flour,
150 pages—I'll need every hour.
a teaspoon of powder—I'm tired, I swear,
a pinch of some soda—does anyone care?
a splash of fresh milk—I'm falling behind,
a dash of vanilla—there's so much on my mind.
beat butter and sugar—I'm feeling so small,
add eggs to the mix—I wonder, am I meant for it all?
a splash of vanilla—rejection again,
fold flour and powder—I fear my dreams are starting to bend.
the soda, some salt—am I even good enough?
whisk milk till it's smooth—I think this climb is too tough.
pour into the tin—I'm scared I might fail,
bake 30 minutes—under duress, I can feel my strength pale.
cut and enjoy—but my heart feels undone,
i'm drowning in an ocean of overwhelming thoughts...
but the cake? it's done.

3. there is poetry in the world around us.

there is poetry in the world around us,
in nature, with sunsets that bathe you in golden ambrosia straight from
the abode of the gods,
sweet, rich, syrupy,
like the golden honey of words strung together.

lush trees, canopies of emerald green fit to sway above the heads of
queens,
protecting, embracing, standing tall,
foreboding, and ever breathing,
the trees will tell generations the stories of us and all those who came
before.

the aquamarine, navy and indigo blue hues of the powerful ocean
waves,
creating the most eclectic melody of soft, gentle laps of the water
against the sand,
and the ferocious roar of the waves in a stormy night.
turbulent, as the human mind,
all conquering, as the human soul.

there is poetry in the world around us,
in humanity, with the soulful wail of the new born babe adjusting to
the harsh light of existence away from the warmth of the womb.

to the glimmer of tears in a mother's eyes watching her children grow,
from saplings to great oaks,
in the harrowing grief in a father's eyes,
watching the destruction of war wreak havoc on his family and life as
he knows it.

in the satisfaction in an authors eyes, when the work of fiction he has
slaved over for years finally weaves together to form a story that pleases
his artistic temperament,
to the soft croon of a guitar, preaching the blues in a dim lit bar.
the smooth symphony of a saxophone, playing softly till long after the
crowds go home.
there is poetry in the world around us,
in creation,
in the masterful strokes of a paintbrush that speak of the greatest
tragedies and glorious histories,
in the perfect swoop of the curve of a statue, evoking the depth of
human beauty,
in the devastating beauty of words coined together to fit just right, to
encapsulate the fact that no matter the era, we have always been the
same.

there is poetry in the world beyond us,
in the cosmos, and it's infinite galaxies of stars, shimmering like
diamonds lighting up the universe in shades of purple and silver.
in the ominous hum of a black hole slowly sucking existence as we
know it towards doomsday,
in the reassurance that the stars that seem ever-glowing and luminant
allow

us to carry stardust in our veins.

there is poetry in the world around us,
and there is beauty in the world around us,
and there is something wonderful in knowing that we assimilate this
beauty into our consciences, knowingly, unknowingly.

there is poetry in the world around us,
pushing us to carpe diem,
pushing us to cogito ergo sum,
forcing us to qui vivra verra.

there is poetry in the world around us,
only if we're brave enough to see it,
strong enough to embrace,
and kind enough to preserve it.

4. it doesn't add up.

I have given everything.
Everything.
Every sleepless night, every breath held in exam halls,
every frantic scribble, every tear-stained page,
every breakdown in the goddamn library bathroom,
pressing my hands against my mouth so no one would hear.

I have sacrificed sleep, sanity,
happiness—
for numbers, for letters,
for something to prove I am worth something.
I have turned my body into a machine,
fed it caffeine and stress,
ignored the shaking hands, the racing heart,
the crushing weight on my chest.

And yet—
it doesn't add up.

I did everything right.
I followed the rules.
I swallowed my fear and kept going,
even when my mind begged me to stop.
I memorized formulas like prayers,
wrote essays until my fingers went numb,

pushed past every limit,
because they said hard work pays off.

And yet—
it doesn't add up.

Tell me why.
Tell me why I watched others stroll into success
while I scraped my knees on the way there.
Tell me why I traded joy for discipline,
why I poured myself into this system
until I was nothing but raw nerves and exhaustion,
for what?

For rejection?
For silence?
For "maybe next time" and "not quite enough"?

Tell me why I measured my worth
in fucking decimal points.
Why I let a grade determine if I was good enough.
Why I crushed myself under this pressure,
praying it would mold me into someone deserving,
only to be left with nothing but

shaking hands and an empty heart.
Tell me why—

because it doesn't add up.

RENA TARA PHOOKAN

•9•

5. time.

a chance meeting,
a rush of memories,
a familiar warmth.

and yet, a curious anxiety,
a lingering ache
an unfamiliar longing.

a flood of nostalgia
a twinge of regret,
a familiar sense of acceptance.

a warm embrace,
a sweet reunion,
and time.
ticking, all encompassing, time.

6. girlhood.

it is in the quiet knowing,
the glance across the room that says, i see you.
in the way hands find each other in the dark,
fingers laced like a lifeline, like a promise.

it is borrowed perfume and shared mirrors,
trading earrings, trading heartaches,
reapplying lip gloss between confessions,
does he love you?
do you love him?
do you love yourself?

it is learning to be soft and sharp at once,
to wield tenderness like armor,
to hold each other through the weight of the world,
because no one else ever taught us how.

it is laughing so hard you can't breathe,
crying so hard you forget why,
knowing you are never alone,
not really,
not when she still texts, home safe?
not when she still carries your secrets in the hollow of her ribs.

girlhood is a hymn we hum together,
a thread we braid between our bones,
a love story without an ending—
a thousand hands, reaching, holding, never letting go.

7. growing up is weird.

growing up is weird.
one day, you can't wait to go home and watch another episode of dora
the explorer.
the next, another episode of friends plays on through a dimly lit screen,
offering more insight into adult life than dora could ever give.
but the lingering want for that comfort stays in the back of your mind,
like a safety blanket, bringing you solace only it can bring.

growing up is weird.
one day, you're begging for five more minutes to play as the sun sets,
grasping at the green grass, muddy knees and sweaty hair clinging to
your cheeks.
the next, you're watching the sun set through a window,
orange hues painting the dark outline of tired eyes,
watching other children run and play and squeal,
and nostalgia floods your bones,
because oh, what you'd give for another round of tag.

growing up is weird.
one day, your biggest problem is who gets the red crayon first,
tears welling up over something as small as a missing sticker.
the next, you're staring at your inbox, waiting for an email that could
change everything,

learning that disappointment doesn't always come in tantrums,
but in quiet sighs and heavy hearts.
growing up is weird.
one day, your parents are the superheroes who know everything,
fixing broken toys and kissing away scraped knees.
the next, you realize they don't have all the answers,
that they are just people too,
figuring things out as they go.
and somehow, that makes you love them even more.

growing up is weird.
one day, you're writing letters to your future self,
dreaming of all the places you'll go and the person you'll become.
the next, you're reading them with teary eyes,
realizing that some dreams change,
some stay the same,
and some slip away before you even notice.

growing up is weird.
because even as you move forward,
even as you take on responsibilities and make big decisions,
there's always a part of you that longs for the past—
for the days when happiness was as simple as a bedtime story,
when love was given freely and without question,
when growing up felt like the most exciting adventure
instead of something that sometimes feels a little too heavy.

but maybe, just maybe,
growing up isn't just about leaving things behind.
maybe it's about carrying those pieces with you,
finding new ways to love,
new ways to dream,
and realizing that some parts of childhood never really leave you.

because growing up is weird.
but it's also kind of beautiful.

8. the weight of a name.

my name sits heavy on my tongue,
a quiet echo of all I am meant to be.
a whisper from my mother's lips,
soft with love, laced with expectation.
a firm call from my father, steady and strong,
a reminder of the legacy I carry.

my name, reshaped by friends,
shortened, stretched, turned into laughter—
a melody of belonging.
my name, murmured by a lover,
gentle, reverent, as if it is sacred.

but some nights, it feels like an anchor,
pulling me down,
reminding me of the weight I must bear—
the dreams I have built, towering,
the fear that I may never reach them.

I am afraid of faltering, of failing,
of proving the quiet voices right,
the ones that whisper in the dark—
what if you are not enough?
what if you never become what they see in you?

I carry my name like a promise,
like a burden, like a prayer.
I try to mold myself to match its strength,
to live up to the person they believe I can be.

and maybe one day,
I will say my name
and feel only pride.

9. wilt and bloom.

I see her in the mirror sometimes—
wide-eyed, sunshine-warmed,
soft laughter slipping between missing teeth,
hope curling in her palms like petals untouched by winter.
She reaches for me,
but I do not know how to hold her anymore.

She was warmth,
all golden hues and wide-open love,
the kind of light that made people linger,
that made the world feel a little softer.
Now, I am something else.
Colder, sharper, quieter.
Not cruel, but cautious.
Not wilted, but weathered

I mourn her like a childhood lullaby,
like the echo of a voice I will never hear again.
She was unafraid.
She believed in forever.
She trusted—oh, how she trusted.
And I?
I have learned too much to be so weightless.

But still, I am growing.
Still, I rise from the ruin,
roots reaching deeper,
petals unfolding, hesitant but sure.
She was the seed,
and I am the bloom.
Different, yes,
but alive all the same.

10. reckless and radiant.

love me like we have forever,
like the world will bend to make room for us,
like the sun wakes just to drench us in gold.
love me with the recklessness of youth,
hands shaking, hearts racing,
like we are the only ones who have ever felt this way.
love me in stolen glances across a crowded room,
in fingers brushing, in laughter that tastes like sugar,
in the kind of silence that hums with something unspoken.
love me like a song you can't shake,
like a wish on an eyelash,
like something fleeting but god—you'd ruin yourself to hold onto it.
love me like it's a secret we'll never tell,
or like we want the whole world to know.
love me like i'm the first person who ever made your hands tremble,
like i'm the only one who ever could.
love me with the foolish, desperate, aching devotion
that only exists before you learn
what it means to lose.

i want it in its loudest, messiest form—
the kind that crashes like a wave and leaves me breathless,
the kind that makes me stupid, reckless,
drunk off the way someone says my name like a prayer.

i want the 2 a.m. confessions,

the hands in my hair, the whispered *stay.*

i want to be someone's first thought, last thought,

the reason their heart stutters in their chest.

i want the unbearable ache of it,

the longing that sits under my skin,

the dizzying, all-consuming, ruinous kind of love

that teenage dreams are made of.

i want to write their name in the margins of my notebooks,

hear a song and pretend it was written about us,

kiss them in the rain just to say i did.

i want love like the movies,

like the books,

like the stories i've swallowed whole

since i was old enough to dream of someone.

i want love to wreck me, rebuild me,

turn me inside out, make me feel—

because anything less would never be enough,

and god, i was *made* to want it all.

11. phantom pain.

grief is not loud.
it is not wailing or falling to the ground.
it is quiet. persistent. patient.
it lingers in the spaces they once stood,
in the half-finished stories they will never get to tell,
in the echo of a voice i can barely remember
but will never forget.

i set the table and still count their chair.
walk into a room and expect to see them,
somewhere in the corner of my eye,
like a trick of the light,
like a cruel joke the universe keeps playing.

grief is muscle memory,
reaching for someone who is no longer there,
saying their name before remembering,
before stopping short,
before swallowing the silence that follows.

people tell me time will soften the edges,
but the ache has settled into my bones.
a wound i have learned to live with,
a shadow i have made space for.
they are gone.

but somehow,
they are still here.

12. paper cuts.

they say pain is loud,
that heartbreak is thunder,
but i have learned
that it is just as often a whisper,
a slow erosion,
a paper-thin slice that doesn't bleed at first—
until you touch it,
until you try to forget.

it is the silence after i speak,
words trailing into nothingness,
as if i was never there at all.
it is the way laughter circles around me,
brushing past but never landing,
the way i fade into the background
until i am nothing but an outline
no one bothers to fill in.

it is standing on the outside,
watching people fold into each other,
belonging without trying,
while i shift my weight from foot to foot,
holding onto words that don't seem to matter.

it is the text left unanswered,
the seat at the table that no one saves,
the way people's eyes glaze past me,
never quite meeting,
never quite seeing.

it is all the little heartbreaks,
too small to grieve,
too sharp to forget.
because some wounds do not come from daggers—
but from the edges of a page,
thin and sharp,
stinging long after the moment has passed.

13. a love letter to tomorrow.

Dear Tomorrow,
I do not know you yet,
but I like to think you are waiting for me
just beyond the horizon,
patient, steady, soft.

today, my hands are heavy,
dragging through the weight of everything unsaid,
of everything I wish I could fix,
of everything I wish I could be.
but you whisper—
not yet, but soon.

you remind me that the oven will hum again,
that butter and sugar will swirl into something sweet,
that the scent of vanilla will wrap itself around me
like a warm embrace.

you remind me that music will play again,
that my voice will rise with the melody,
that I will sing, not for anyone else,
but for myself,
because I was made for joy.

you remind me that books will wait with open arms,
their pages ready to take me somewhere else,
to stories where love and courage win,
where even the lost find their way home.

you remind me that family laughter will fill the kitchen,
that familiar voices will call my name,
that love, in its simplest form,
is a movie night, a shared meal,
a hand reaching for mine across the table.

and so, I hold on.
because even when today feels like too much,
you are there, waiting,
whispering promises in the quiet—
not yet, but soon.

and that is enough.

14. golden hour.

for a moment, just a moment,
I am bathed in gold.

the sun drapes itself over my skin,
melting into my hair,
threading soft honey through each strand,
tracing light against my cheekbones
as if the universe itself
is painting me in warmth.

amber spills across my hands,
a quiet glow,
like molten light pooling in my palms,
turning my fingertips to gold.
I tilt my face to the sky,
and the world hums—
soft, slow, golden.

for a moment, just a moment,
I see myself the way the sun does—
not in harsh fluorescents,
not in the glare of mirrors,
not through the eyes of others,
but in warmth,
in light,

in something fleeting,
but still so beautiful.

and maybe I am.

15. cosmic serendipity.

somewhere, light-years away,
a star flickers out, dust scattering,
shimmering remnants drifting across the universe—
perhaps to land here,
softly, quietly, in the space between us.

fate is an odd thing, isn't it?
a million little chances,
a thousand moments that could have gone another way,
but didn't.
and somehow, in this vast, endless cosmos,
i found *you.*

you, who laugh with me until our sides ache,
who see me when the world turns away,
who make me feel like i was never meant to be invisible.
you, who remind me that i am not a whisper,
but a constellation—*burning, radiant, infinite.*

you, who built me a universe of love,
who anchor me in the quiet certainty
that i have always been wanted,
long before i even knew how to ask for it.

the world is chaos, spinning, relentless,
but in this mess of entropy and chance,
somehow, the universe conspired in my favor.
somehow, i was given you.

and isn't that magic?

for my family and closest friends.

16. sepia toned ghosts.

there are echoes of me in every place I have left behind,
faint silhouettes of the girl I used to be,
pressed into old journals, tucked between yellowed pages,
lingering in the walls of childhood bedrooms,
in the way the wind hums through familiar streets.

I see her sometimes,
in the way I hesitate before speaking,
in the instinct to shrink, to soften, to make myself small.
she is the girl who once apologized for existing,
the one who mistook silence for safety,
who thought love had to be earned.

another one lingers in the mirror,
a version of me who dared to dream,
who carried stars in her hands but was too afraid to let them burn.
I wonder if she knew
that I would one day learn to hold fire without flinching,
that I would grow into a voice that did not tremble,
a presence that did not waver.

and yet, there are others still—
bright-eyed ghosts who laughed too loudly,
who danced without shame,
who believed in magic with the unwavering certainty of a child.

I ache for them the most,

for their sunlight, their sweetness, their softness,

for the way they loved the world before it taught them how to hurt.

but I do not mourn them.

They are not lost, only layered beneath the skin of who I have become.

I am every version of myself that has ever existed,

folded into one, like pressed flowers in an old book,

not faded—just transformed.

17. the softest war.

girlhood is a quiet battlefield,
a war waged in whispers and glances,
in the way our knees are told to stay unbruised,
our voices to stay gentle,
our anger to stay hidden.

it is sugar-laced warnings,
a lady smoothing my dress, saying,
"sit like a lady."
it is the weight of a name spoken with expectation,
the curve of a body seen before the mind is ready,
the lesson that smiling is safer than saying no.

girlhood is running barefoot through sunlit streets,
scraped elbows and wild laughter,
before the world teaches us
that softness can be dangerous,
that growing up means growing quiet.

it is learning to shrink before you understand why,
to apologize for taking up space,
to carry the unspoken rules like second skin.

but girlhood is also late-night secrets,
whispered dreams over tangled hands,

the unbreakable bond of sisterhood,
the fire beneath soft words,
the resilience woven into every *no*,
every dream too bold to be silenced.

girlhood is the softest war,
but we are warriors still.

18. epiphany.

it comes to me in a whisper,
soft as the hush of the ocean at dawn,
a knowing, a truth, a quiet revelation
wrapped in the arms of time.

epiphany is the weight of a suitcase,
the realization that home is not four walls,
but the voices that call you back,
the laughter that lingers in empty spaces.

epiphany is the way the past lingers,
in the scent of monsoon-soaked earth,
in the worn pages of a childhood book,
in the echo of a song you no longer remember learning.

epiphany is understanding that love is in the details—
in a mother's hands, weathered but warm,
in a father's silent gestures,
in the way a friend remembers how you take your tea.

epiphany is watching the sunset and knowing—
the world keeps turning, and so will you.
epiphany is realizing that growing up is not about leaving behind,
but about carrying forward.

it is a moment, a breath, a heartbeat—
and then,
it is everything.

19. weightless.

I close my eyes, and the world softens,
blurring into something golden and endless.
the weight I have carried for so long—
the should-haves, the what-ifs, the never-weres—
melts like morning mist beneath the sun.

for the first time in forever,
I am light.
drifting, untethered, free.
not lost, not found—just existing,
exactly as I am, exactly as I should be.

there is no rush, no race, no destination.
only the steady hum of the universe,
the slow exhale of the wind through the trees,
the quiet assurance that I am here,
and that is enough.

maybe this is peace.
maybe this is what it means to be alive.

20. silver and shattered light.

I have learned to be what the world wants,
to spin, to shimmer, to glow just right.
a thousand tiny pieces of me
reflecting what they need to see,
never whole, but always shining.

I twirl beneath the weight of watching eyes,
turning myself into something beautiful,
something easy to love,
something that catches the light
just enough to make you stay.

but when the music slows, when the room empties,
who am I in the quiet?
do I still glimmer without an audience?
do I still matter when no one is watching?

the truth is—I will always shine.
not for them, not for you,
but because I was made of light
long before I learned to bend it.

and even if I fall, even if I break,
I will still scatter silver across the floor,

a constellation of all the times
I tried to be everything
and somehow, still,
remained me.

21. to the ones who refuse to bow.

There is a storm in our voices,
a fire that no empire can extinguish.
They built their towers high,
etched their names in stone,
believing history belongs only to the hands that hold the pen.
But we are the ink,
the ones who rewrite the story,
who turn whispers into war cries,
who do not kneel before thrones carved from stolen power.

They say, "This is the way things have always been."
But we are the ones who ask, "Why?"
We are the ones who dare to dream beyond the chains of tradition,
who see the cracks in the foundation and know
that even the mightiest walls will crumble
when enough hands push against them.

Justice is not given—it is taken,
pulled from clenched fists,
ripped from the grip of those who hoard it.
We are not here to beg,
to wait for mercy like crumbs from their feast.
We are here to break the table,
to build something better,

to ensure that no one is left starving at the gates.

They call us reckless, ungrateful, too loud.
But we are only as loud as the silence they forced upon us.
Only as unyielding as the weight we have carried.
Only as dangerous as truth in the face of their lies.

So let them tremble.
Let them curse our names in fear.
For we are the storm,
the reckoning,
the dawn of a world they swore would never come.

And we will not stop.
Not until every chain is broken,
every voice is heard,
every soul stands free beneath a sky
that belongs to *all of us*.

22. the manifesto of a dreamer.

I have lived a thousand lives in the quiet corners of my mind,
built empires from nothing but whispered dreams
and painted futures in colors no one else could see.
the world told me to be realistic,
but reality has never been enough for me.

I have dreamed of revolutions born in libraries,
of cities where kindness is currency,
of hands reaching across borders,
tearing down walls like paper castles in the wind.
I have seen a world where no one is left behind,
where justice is not a privilege,
but the air we all breathe.

but dreams alone cannot carry us forward—
they are the spark, not the fire.
there is work to be done between the poetry and the protest,
between the vision and the bricks we lay down with tired hands.
change is not just in the dreaming,
but in the slow, steady steps toward something better.

and so, I walk the line between stars and soil,
between the boundless sky and the weight of the earth.
I let my head drift among the constellations,

but my feet remain steady on the ground,
learning when to fight like a storm
and when to build like the tide,
slow, relentless, unstoppable.

because the world does not bend easily,
but I was never meant to break.
And maybe I will not see the revolutions I dream of,
but I will lay the foundation
so that one day, someone else will.

for the dreamers and the builders,
for those who refuse to choose between hope and action—
we are the ones who shape tomorrow.

23. fate vs free will

They said the stars had already spoken,
whispered my fate in constellations inked across the sky,
as if I were nothing but a footnote in the script of the universe,
as if my hands weren't made for tearing pages,
for redrawing maps, for carving a path of my own.
I was told to follow the road well-tread,
to heed the omens, to bow before destiny's decree—
but what is fate, if not a tale left unfinished?
What is prophecy, if not a challenge to defy?
I will not be a passenger in my own life.
I will not wait for the winds to carry me
or for the stars to grant me permission to shine.
My story is mine to write,
each word an act of defiance,
each breath a declaration of freedom.
Let the universe watch in awe
as I shape my own destiny,
as I become the author of my own becoming.

24. the art of creation.

it begins as a whisper,
a flicker of something not yet whole,
half-formed and trembling in the quiet.
a thought, a brushstroke, a chord, a line—
each one reaching for something bigger,
something just out of grasp.

creation is a battle,
a dance between chaos and clarity,
between the fear of imperfection
and the thrill of possibility.
it is ink-stained hands and sleepless nights,
the gnawing ache of doubt
and the stubborn defiance to try anyway.

it is chiseling at the marble,
trusting that something beautiful
lurks beneath the stone.
it is the blank page staring back,
daring you to fill it with something true.

and yet, in the midst of the struggle,
there is magic—
in the moment a melody finds its home,
in the way colors melt into each other,

in the words that finally, finally feel right.

to create is to become,
to shape something from nothing,
to leave a mark that says:
I was here. I imagined. I made. I lived.

25. ticking away

time is a thief dressed in silence,
slipping through our fingers like sand,
marking its presence not in moments,
but in the spaces between them—
the missed calls, the forgotten names,
the way childhood fades before you even realize
it was something you were supposed to hold on to.

the clock does not wait for wisdom,
nor does it pity the dreamer
who swore they had more of it to waste.
the sun rises, the sun sets,
the hands keep moving forward,
indifferent to how much we beg them to slow.

and yet—
there is beauty in knowing
that nothing stays the same.
that every sunrise is a little different,
that every breath is a new beginning,
that even as we race towards an end
we cannot outrun,
we are, for this moment,
here.

so *laugh*, even as the echoes fade.
love, even as the years strip us bare.
create, even as time warns you
that nothing is permanent.
because if everything must pass,
let it pass knowing
you left something behind.

26. academic validation.

i wonder if i exist beyond numbers,
beyond the red ink and weighted scores,
beyond the quiet nods of approval
that only come when i perform.

am i more than the sleepless nights,
more than the margins filled with frantic notes,
more than the way my worth
seems to shrink and expand
with every result?

i chase perfection like it's the only road forward,
like it will carve my name into something lasting,
but i fear the cost of being seen only in the light
of what i achieve,
not who i am.

tell me, would you still think i am brilliant
if i set down my pen,
if i let myself breathe,
if i existed just to be—
not to prove?

because i am more than the sum of my grades,
more than the pressure curling in my chest,

more than the hunger for validation
that i was taught to call ambition.

i am the books i love,
the music that moves me,
the way my laughter sounds in the right company.
i am whole, even when the world
only measures the parts of me
it finds useful.

27. the language of love.

It is in the hand that lingers a moment longer,
the quiet look across a crowded room,
the way a mother hums to her child,
the way a friend waits in the rain.

It is whispered in every language,
braided into every history,
written in letters never sent,
carved into tree trunks that outlive the hands that held the knife.

It hums in the hush of a temple,
soars in the chorus of a song,
blooms between strangers who meet at the right time,
or the wrong time,
but love them anyway.

It is the tether between souls who have never met,
the echo of laughter in an empty house,
the grief that proves something was once whole.

It is old as the first heartbeat,
as young as the next confession,
a story retold in every life,
but never the same twice.

It is the crack in the armor,
the surrender in a held breath,
the quiet mercy of being truly seen.

It is terrifying in its gentleness,
a force that bends and breaks,
that shakes the earth without a sound.

It is the hand that reaches first,
the voice that says, stay,
the choice made over and over again,
even when it would be easier to turn away.

It does not promise safety,
does not ask for perfection,
only that you let it in—
that you let it change you.

It will ruin you,
it will save you.
It will demand everything,
and give back more.

It is the only thing that makes the waiting worth it,
the aching bearable,
the fleeting—eternal.

28. canvas.

golden mornings drip honey over the world,
spilling light through windows, warm and slow,
a quiet promise that today holds something new,
something waiting to be seen.

emerald leaves whisper in the wind,
spinning secrets in soft rustling tones,
a lullaby for those who stop to listen,
for those who remember to breathe.

the ocean hums in blues and indigo,
pulling in hearts that ache for infinity,
for the vastness, for the unbroken rhythm,
for the feeling of being small but endless.

red pulses through fingertips, through veins,
in laughter, in rage, in passion that cannot be contained.
It is the color of all things felt deeply,
of love that lingers, of wounds that heal.

soft lavender dusk settles on tired shoulders,
a gentle hush, a fading song,
the sky melting into itself,
a reminder that even endings can be beautiful.

and in between, we exist—
blushing pink with fleeting joy,
spilling silver tears in quiet rooms,
glowing amber in the warmth of another's touch.

we are a canvas of shifting hues,
a painting never quite finished,
a masterpiece in motion.

29. passion.

I want to live like wildfire—
untamed, relentless, burning bright,
devouring fear with every breath,
setting the night ablaze with hunger.

I want love that crashes like waves,
fierce, aching, all-consuming,
pulling me under only to lift me higher,
a tide that never recedes.

I want to chase dreams with bloody hands,
fingertips raw from gripping the impossible,
lungs filled with the sharp air of risk,
eyes blazing with the thrill of more.

I want to stand where the world cracks open,
where stars pour into the earth,
where every heartbeat is a battle cry,
and every step is a leap into the unknown.

Give me fire, give me fury,
give me a life that dares to burn—
let me be the storm,
let me be the spark,
let me be *alive.*

30. searching for me.

whoever you are, searching for me,
know that I have already slipped through your fingers—
a breath of wind, a shifting tide,
never still long enough to be held.

you may trace the lines of my hands,
but they will rewrite themselves by morning.
you may press my name into your tongue,
but it will taste different each time you say it.

do not try to know me as something fixed,
as something that can be named and kept—
for I am a wildfire and a quiet stream,
a ghost of who I was yesterday,
a stranger to who I will be tomorrow.

whoever you are, trying to keep me,
know that I was never meant to stay.
I am the girl with wild feet and restless hands,
with a heart that beats in untamed rhythms,
always chasing the next horizon.

you may try to catch me in a name,
but I will outgrow the sound of it.
you may try to pin me to a moment,

but I will slip through time like water through open palms.

I am not meant to be understood,
not by you, not even by myself.
only witnessed, only felt—
like the sky before a storm,
like a bird that does not ask where it is going,
only trusts the wind to take it there.

do not ask me to be still,
to fold myself into something small and knowable.
I am a storm that changes shape mid-fall,
a fire that learns new ways to burn.

I will always be becoming,
always unlearning, unraveling,
braiding myself into someone new.
and maybe you will love me anyway,
not for what I was, not for what I will be,
but for the girl who refuses to be anything
but free.

31. letting go.

the day soon approaches
when i have to let go of the only lifestyle I've ever known.
when i must step out of my home,
onto the soil of another temporary home,
one that calls me far away from those that i love.
the day soon approaches,
when I will have to pack all 18 years of my belongings into a small
suitcase and wonder how on earth I'll make everything fit.
when I will have to pick which of my favourite outfits will make it
with me,
which of the ugly comfort t shirts will be there for the nights when the
dorm seems just a little too cold.
the day soon approaches,
when I will have to step out of my door, go down the 33 steps to the
ground floor and then not turn back.
when I will have to ask my friends "wanna go get lunch tomorrow?"
one last time before we all head off on new paths
when I will give tight hugs and make tender promises to my day ones
that I will return as soon as I can.
the day soon approaches that I will watch my dad tell me quietly to
take my medicines with me, because he won't be around if I need him
out of the blue.
when my mother and I will have a temporary last mother daughter
bonding conversation and she will tell me she will miss my dramatics.

the day my brother will look at me and say gruffly "i guess I'll miss you"
the day soon approaches when I will step into a terminal, take a look at my family, and feel a piece of my heart begin to ache.
when I will try to keep the tears at bay as I roll that one 25 kg suitcase into the airport, my whole army of a family behind me, all fighting back tears.
when I will put on a brave face but my mother will see the tears well up in my eyes.
the day soon approaches that I will leave this place I have called home for 18 years to start new beginnings and follow my dreams.
and I will let go.
only for a moment.
before i hold on again.
tighter than ever before.

32. reverie.

I slip between waking and dreaming,
adrift in the space where memories blur,
where time folds like worn pages,
and I am every version of myself at once.

I am the child with skinned knees,
chasing fireflies through the thick summer air,
laughter bubbling like a song I have since forgotten.
I am the teenager staring at the ceiling,
wondering if the world will ever make space for me,
if my voice will ever feel loud enough.

I am the echo of unfinished conversations,
the quiet goodbyes that never found their words,
the ghosts of almosts and could-have-beens,
lingering like dust caught in the golden light.

I wander through old dreams like a house I once lived in,
tracing my fingers over the walls,
finding pieces of myself I thought I had lost.

And maybe that is the truth of it—
that we never truly leave behind the people we were,
that we are stitched together from every fleeting moment,
every dream half-remembered,

every longing that never quite faded.

In the end, I am nothing more than a reverie,
a collection of whispers, of echoes, of light—
but oh, how beautiful it is to exist in between.

Adieu

to those who have stayed till the last page, you have my thanks.

to those who feel they resonate, you have my love.

to those who simply *feel*, you have the greatest gift of all : <u>empathy.</u>